I0115730

ON INACCURACY

An Essay

by Joe Manning

C&R Press
Conscious & Responsible

Winter Soup Bowl Chapbook 2017
Second Collection
Selection 2 of 2 CB7

All Rights Reserved

Printed in the United States of America

First Edition
1 2 3 4 5 6 7 8 9

Selections of up to two pages may be reproduced without permissions. To reproduce more than two pages of any one portion of this book write to C&R Press publishers John Gosslee and Andrew Sullivan.

Cover Design by Sally Underwood
Interior Design by Ali Chica

Copyright ©2017 by Joseph Manning

ISBN: 978-1-936196-76-0

C&R Press
Conscious & Responsible
www.crpress.org

For special discounted bulk purchases please contact:
C&R Press sales@crpress.org

Thank you to our generous Patreon patrons.

ON INACCURACY

In My Eyes

All the kids at St. Agnes School took an eye exam once a year in the library. We looked into anvil-black microscopes while a technician said things like, "Now close your right eye and tell me what you see." Backlit inside, slides of predictable shapes and colors needed to be sorted out and described. It seemed like a game and, growing up with an older brother and sister, I did not lose games gracefully. So, I cheated on the eye test. I juked it. Opened one eye on the sly, guessed and intuited. I got the answers right and 20/20 with a check-mark next to it as proof. The procedure that was intended to assess the visual acuity of a bunch of children was a breeze and I considered myself a winner.

I was an adult before I discovered that, at 20/400, I am, and have likely always been, legally blind in my left eye. I was partial to my particular brand of visual perception by the time I learned this. It seems to work well enough. I'm an excellent driver. When I wore glasses for about a week once, the world looked like it had been filmed in cinematic 3-D which is to say novel, but decidedly unconvincing. The doctors tell me I'm myopic, an accusation I object to in the utmost, greatly preferring the diagnosis put forth by a teacher who told me years ago, "You have an interesting way of looking at things." Damn right.

The difference between seeing and looking is nuanced. I've thought about it. A pretty quotidian distinction suggests the difference to be a matter of intentionality: one might walk through the woods and see a pile of feathers that was formerly a bird before it was mauled by a fox, but you have to bend down and *look* real close at the downy gore to identify the yellow, pencil-wide tips of a cedar wax-wing's tail feathers. You don't *see* for something, you *look* for something.

All the same, cache is given to the act of seeing over the act of looking. One need look no further than our definition of, and classical associations with the word *seer*, which, as far as Middle English etymology goes, is about as easy as it gets: See+er and, bam, you're done. A seer can allegedly *see* beyond the veil of illusion to the world as it really is. Seeing bears a connotation of unfiltered perceptive accuracy. The rightness of sight is the gospel laid bare, and we are converted souls, even while our belief is challenged and refuted at every turn. Is there no value to inaccuracy?

In pictures, I appear to have a lazy eye. My good eye looks straight and true into the camera, confident that the cones and rods distributing light into my visual cortex as electro-chemical impulses are—in some very essential regard—accurately representing the world around me. The other eye hangs back a little, unconvinced. "I don't know," my left eye seems to say. "Maybe."

I've never addressed the issue of my allegedly poor vision. I was told that wearing an eye-patch over my good eye might strengthen the ocular muscles in my weak one a little. I did not where an eye-patch. But, the idea that my sight could become stronger by withholding information interested me, and I've spent the better part of twenty years thinking about this remedy in broader existential terms. If covering my good eye could strengthen the perception in my weak eye, I have reasoned, could it be that some hidden faculties in my perception were being strengthened by and compensating for that weakness already? Is it possible that my cognition learned to fill in the blank spaces left by my blindness by establishing correlations? Really, the question that I've been laboring to determine the last two decades is this: Could my blindness itself be thought of as an organ of impression?

Old blind-ass Tireisius was a seer and a walking tragedy who could scarcely help himself. His foresight, like his blindness, was a curse to him. He was cursed by the Gods blind. I'm just legally blind and opt not to wear corrective lenses. This makes me either a low-rent conscientious objector or a petty criminal by comparison. There are seekers and seers and watchers and viewers. I'm just a looker.

In The Viewfinder

We'd come to Northern Michigan for my girlfriend Joan's family reunion. Her forbears were a gang of mutton-chopped, frock-coated 19th century brothers who made glass jars, and theirs is a family of an intergenerational, industrial stripe you don't see much anymore, one that succeeded by producing a simple object people needed and bought. Her ancestors doubled down, expanded, and succeeded the old fashioned way. Every decade their descendants, two hundred of them now, get together for a barn dance hoedown, a golf-scramble, and a cocktail cruise on Lake Michigan in a big gray ferry rented by the hour. This year they had a small boat race on Lake Leelanau too.

I watched the sailboat race for a while through a big brass telescope like the ones at the Grand Canyon that tend to be out of order, the ones that look like a flat-faced owl with little hoods over the peepholes. Tiny dimples hammered into the front amplified the bird effect and, from a distance, looked like a coat of downy crown feathers. I'll run clear out of my way to look through these things. It's an irrepressible compulsion, actually. When they're out of operation, though, when you look inside only onto flat blackness, you get a little coin-slot heartbreak, a regret for what might have been seen: a nickel going click but nothing delivered. When they work, though, you get to look and see.

I stood up on the concrete pedestal, put my eyes up to the owl's and got a whiff of the light blue tang of oxidized metal, what a lightbulb filament must smell like in the cold. The coin slot was disabled, so shaky views of Lake Leelanau were free. Inside the viewer, two flat, distorted circles of action floated beside one another ringed in black, two shaking circles that replicated the same little boats rallying and capsizing. The perspectives in the two lenses were synchronous and sympathetic. But they were also essentially independent from one another, as if two worlds, indistinguishable in nearly every regard, had been laid somewhat carelessly on top of one another, hyper-real and only half collaborating. They shimmied hesitantly against one another like dancers who've tired of standing on the wall waiting for a partner.

I'd never watched a single-hand sailboat regatta, or any regatta for that matter. Regatta is a good word—beautiful in the eye and in the ear. It comes from the Venetian Italian for "contention for mastery" and, as such, bore little resemblance to the splashing cacophony I saw out there amidst the white-then-charcoal-green breakers on the lake, and the unintelligible signals blasted on a bullhorn. I assumed that the boats had a purpose in their movement, but it wasn't evident from where I stood. Viewed as a whole with my naked eye, as one act, the race was as impenetrable as watching starlings etching impossible shapes in the sky. I didn't know the rules, or what was supposed to be happening. The lines they traveled were their own; their tacks and sallies were not for me to understand.

But in the closed unevenness of the viewfinder, my sight was no longer burdened by the unruliness of the crowd, and I watched a few individual sailors whose individual trajectories could be followed. What I saw in the viewfinder and what I could perceive with my naked eye were two worlds operating on top of one another. The actions of both perspectives, the unruly and the discreet, were taking place simultaneously, and I—the looker—admired the view and the imprecision of both.

In Photographs

The weekend's main event was a big barn-dance hoedown. At twilight, we drove up to a cherry orchard and a picture-postcard red barn with white trim. The light and the length of the day said it was June, but we needed our coats. Joan and I arrived just in time for the group photo. By just in time I mean that, even though we were clearly late, it took an hour to get the other 200 people in their places. Children and old folk can be difficult to wrangle, camera lenses can be difficult to wrangle, and the photographer was made to stand on a ladder and use her outside voice once or twice to corral everyone out of their cups and into the frame. The idea of this photograph, of all group portraits really, was to prove for posterity that this family had been together once, to put a pin in time and mark a moment as noteworthy. Photographs remember us for ourselves, to ourselves. Family portraits make a "self" of a community, for people who may never know one another.

At somebody else's family reunion you're on good behavior, and I walked around the barn on ancient pine floorboards listening with actual, not feigned, interest to old aunties, bushwhacking, outlaw cousins, a great uncle who's the last of the old guard, and a young cousin who would've been a writer but was tapped to run the family business, who told me where they'd come from and how their people had arrived in that barn. Reunions are an exercise in shared historical collaboration where we continue telling ourselves stories that were started on our behalf, adding footnotes, and sketching drafts of new entries. You could call it group self-mythologizing, but you'd only be half-right. Reunions are, as much as we are capable, a personal activation of and integration with history. Reunions are active interactions that allow us to participate with our past, to look at ourselves in a narrative that stretches beyond our own and situate us in a "self" with a longer view.

At my own family reunion a few years back someone showed up with a box of glass slides and an antique stereoscope viewer. The instrument's forced dimensional perspective relies on a trick in which two photographs of the same subject are taken from slightly different angles and transferred to a slide next to each other: one for each eye. The effect was similar to the red, plastic Fischer-Price viewer I had as a kid only clearer and, of course, featuring my family inside, instead of cartoons, Old Faithful, or the Statue of Liberty.

"Wow," and "damn" were the most common refrains as each of us took turns staring into the rooms of my family's ancestral home: a white colonial with plain, delicate appointments in Frankfort, Kentucky. A series of pictures showed my father, his brothers, and his sister around a Christmas tree, or by the hearth, in various states of play and formal dress. The clarity of the forced perspective was astonishing—the past rendered as a physical space with depth and gravity—and my eyes were convinced for an instant that those rooms from sixty years ago could still be occupied, a face touched, a shirt tucked in, a curl put back into place. There was a strong dose of the uncanny in there, and the finality of what happened before, the conclusiveness of the past, was momentarily obscured in film stock that bathed and coddled its subjects in brassy hues of the type that immediately elicits a general, object-less nostalgia; I've spent years trying to account for this effect

I shoved the thing at my Uncle Pete, a big man whose humor—dry, prompt, and largely without edits—operates like an old-fashioned punch-card computing machine: feed Pete a subject and, in the blink of an eye, funny and usually jarring insight is spit back at you whether you asked for it or not. Pete looked inside the stereoscope for a moment, took a loud breath through his nose, looked for another moment, then handed it back to me, staring into the middle distance of recollection, saying only, "That's deep, brother." It was like the past had jumped out of the thing, grabbed him by his neck, and chilled the humor out of him entirely. Uncle Pete was older after having looked through that tunnel at what came before, and I felt some kind of regret, like I'd done him a disservice.

Proust's *Remembrance of Things Past* has also been translated as *In Search of Lost Time*. The dissonance in these translations rubs one inscrutable concept against another, and a scent is transferred. We'd often prefer *not* to remember, *not* to go searching, and just as often, "lost" feels like a natural, anonymous, convenient resting place for the past. Discomfiting though they may sometimes be, our interactions with the past serve as a tether that locates us in the present moment. *Something* just happened; here we are.

The hand-hewn posts and beams that bore the load of the barn at Joan's family reunion were carved in spots with graffiti—*someone loves someone 1934*—etched with slender pocket knives back when pockets still had room for knives. Looking at them, tracing my fingers across the words, interpreting their meaning as something so common, the past was called back to answer and offered a measure of reassurance that what came before is, in some essential regard, responsible for the present moment. Someone-who-loved-someone in 1934 had grandbabies dancing on the floorboards of that room. I find it reassuring to be reminded that this moment—the one we're living every second, second, second—has a mooring somewhere.

Daguerreotypes had been set on shelves and tables throughout the barn, and clusters the family hung around the photos talking, pointing, recalling, collaborating. I studied the minutia of an image featuring a woman holding her infant. The mother had plated her black hair into a gentle, flat semi-circle on the left side of her face and wore a white, crinoline dress buttoned all the way up to a lace collar. In her life outside that photograph, her skin would have retained some sepia, the color of an almond or the tip of a dry pine needle. I lingered for a moment inside a consideration of the obvious, that, before they were American immigrants, immigrants were from someplace else. The bones in her face, suggested a time that is not now. I had, again, this inscrutable feeling that some facial structures are just no longer with us. Where did *that* style of human face go? Where did *that* cheek-to-chin-bone ratio disappear to? Lost in the recessive forests of the hinterlands?

The thought was barely formed in my mind when I turned to discover that it had not gone anywhere. It was intact, and perfectly recognizable in that same barn, in one entire side of Joanie's family. I gestured to an elegant woman across the room and said to Joan, "She's related to this lady in the photograph, right?" Her second cousin's cheekbones were high on her face, her eyes dark as maple sap, skin the color of a toasted almond. The past was present and accounted for.

The exposure time on those early cameras was so long that if someone blinked, a ghostly film covered their eyes in the final image. Blink your eyes and you're a ghost.

In The Pines

If you're American and have eaten four cherries in your life, three of them came from Leelanau County, Michigan. The climate's perfect for a cherry tree and the place is covered up in orchards. During the harvest season, you can't drive more than a mile without seeing a little Norman Rockwell road-side shack—old wagon wheels and potted flowers and all—where you can pull over for a bag of fresh cherries. Nobody works these stands. Customers leave their five bucks in a little wooden box for payment. You'd call it the honor system, but the pay-boxes all have padlocks on them. Speculative honor system, then. Honor practiced with some caveats.

Driving through the county, views of the lake appear out of nowhere like deer or possum. It's distracting and breathtaking. You have to be careful not to wreck; staggering natural beauty can be dangerous even at modest speeds. Drive responsibly though, and you'll come around a wooded bend and be safely overwhelmed by wide views across hill and orchard that continue on and over until they fall off the edge into a place that looks like the ocean. The sweep and lay of the topography is crossed by straight rows at perfect intervals, a calm, orderly composition of balance bordered on all sides by wilderness.

For about a million years before it was cherry orchards, the county was covered with mixed mesophytic forests dominated by Michigan and white pines. Hundreds of thousands of acres. A million maybe. By the turn of the century, the landscape was timbered to within an inch of its life and folks like to say that, after the fire, Chicago was rebuilt with lumber from Leelanau. While the old growth is gone for good, huge tracts of forest have grown back and, hiking through the woods near the lake, I can never avoid the sensation that I've stepped back into a pre-colonial wilderness. Maybe it's the height of the pines, the way the ground is so soft, shaded, and quiet under foot. It's a cloistered and protected place. It's hidden. Sometimes the woods are so dark during the day that it's like being inside.

We walked over a few densely wooded hills to Lake Michigan every day on a path that terminated atop a small cliff overlooking Lake Michigan. There's a break in the trees where bowed limbs make a sort of proscenium arch, and the lake is presented like a stage-show; all that's missing is the curtain. I like to sit on a bench there and look at the horizon line bisecting the water and the sky. When it's overcast out, the whitecap-flecked gray of the lake and the cirrus-streaked gray above are nearly indistinguishable. It's all just a study in gray.

I'm not often *in the moment*, as the saying goes; my mind refracts and bends thoughts like light in a faceted lens: one association reflecting and illuminating another, recursively. It's exhausting. If there were any place in the world to just *be*, without the interruption of interpretation, it would be on that bench. Still, every time we get to the end of the path and I see the lake through the proscenium trees, I imagine an American Indian looking out and glimpsing Europeans for the first time. The place forces a consideration of the Colonies, and I project the image of a square-rigger out in the lake and try to elicit a response from the fictional Native I'm playing. My character lacks any practicable knowledge of ocean going sail ships, though, and his mind conjures an explanation for the shapes in the distance: a giant bird, like an enormous swan, floating in a place that was, until this moment, very familiar to him.

In paintings recounting the first meeting between American Indians and Columbus, white folk in dazzling breeches stand erect on a beach, clustered around a billowing standard, the cross of Columbus planted in the ground on behalf of Ferdinand ever and anon. The Indians are spread out in these compositions and are represented in various states of surprise and goodwill; some on their knees, penitent before they'd had a chance to learn what penitence really means, others welcoming the strangers, shaking hands with their new white brothers, clapping the shoulders of their destroyers. There are always a few Indians somewhere in the tree line though, over in the bushes, covering their eyes. One cups both hands over his temples. In the parlance of contemporary body language, the gesture is precisely equivalent to a posture that says, simply, "…Fuck."

That guy's the only one in the painting who knows what's about to go down. This is what I think of when I think of representative art.

On The Beach

The beaches are lined with houses now. As much as is possible, they all look onto the lake. I never spent any time in lake towns growing up and was confused at first by the orientation of the homes, none of which faced the road in a way I was accustomed to. Driving around a lake town feels, to me, like one continuous, very beautiful, alley; It's like doing laps in a corridor that continuously hints at a greater revelation somewhere out of sight. When you get a glimpse of the lake through the pines it all makes sense, all that focus on vantage and perspective.

At any time of year, but mostly in the summer and fall, the carcasses of cormorants, gulls, and other water fowl can be found rotting in the dune grass or out on the open beach, partially buried in the sand, sticks in their eyes and mouths, opened up in places a living creature couldn't tolerate. A twenty or thirty-minute walk will turn up a dozen dead birds at least. If you have a dog with you—every single time, without fail—they'll sniff around into the birds, dig a snout down in the unseemly stasis of a corpse that— perhaps more than any other species of corpse—is out place. The flesh of the birds, the muscles and guts, rot quickly, but the feathers are designed for the weather and the air, and so they are persistent.

You have to yell at a dog to stop him sniffing and digging at the dead birds. That type of yelling is a pitiful noise, no match for the sounds of the waterfront: the tide and the wind in the dune grass. It's unnatural to yell in someplace like that, not for the sake of propriety or sanctity. It's just too small a noise, unwelcome as it is ineffective.

The birds are dead with botulism. The bacteria occurs naturally in the sediment at the bottom of the lake where it's held in check by cold temperatures and by the low levels of oxygen, the same anaerobic environment that can preserve sunken timbers indefinitely. Rising water temperatures and the appearance in the last sixty years or so of an invasive fish, the Round gobo, have disrupted a balance. The gobo has a broad tolerance for temperatures and cruises up and down through the strata of the lake. As they're eaten up by bigger fish, the pestilence is taken with the gobo—all the way up the food chain—until larger fish are floating on the surface, or are dying, stupefied, just underneath, a meal too easy to pass up for birds with acute, hungry vision. The fish and the birds are equalized there, in the middle, in the flat line of the horizon, brought together in a place of mutual stasis. As above, so below, the botulism go where the gobo go.

We talk about invasive species in terms of being, "out of place," or "not belonging here." It's a predictable response to change but is, if not actually inaccurate, at least the victim of aesthetic sensibilities more appropriate to gardeners and museum curators. These perceptions rely on doting, idyllic concepts of nature that we employ in poetry and song when sometimes what's called for are clear-eyed assessments. Nature operates in deep time, and its movements are above our pay grade. Humans are also an invasive species, but one with the capacity to question the wisdom of its movements in hindsight. We are capable of malice and regret, tolerance, and beauty and stupidity. And with a half-blind sense of our impact, we're just starting to understand the idea that we've shit the global, ecological bed. Our movements are as natural now as the end of our movements will be by and by.

I'll warrant that this is something of an academic argument as everything on the planet goes haywire and birds fall out of the fucking sky.

In The Wilderness

I was in the kitchen with Joan's brother, John Michael. He was making tea and I was reading. We were enjoying the type of silence-in-close-proximity afforded to people with a mutual regard for quiet and a fondness for one another just strong enough to take that quiet for a test drive. Our communal solitude was interrupted by weird, harried sounds of disbelief and concern from Joan outside.

"You guys! Get out here right now!" The exclamation mark doesn't really cover it. She was upset.

I scare easily. I have wondered if this isn't another consequence of my poor eyesight. The evolutionary development of human visual acuity is thought to be related to the threat of animals—poisonous snakes for instance—that are difficult to see in the wild. Knowledge of the serpent made us better lookers, and folks whose eyes could spot a snake in the grass avoided being killed by them. Those folks passed the genetic predisposition for visual acuity on to their babies, and so on. My jumpiness, then, may be a coping mechanism for my bum eye. Maybe I'm just constitutionally jumpy though. John Michael and I bounded down the heart pine steps, shooed the dogs inside and followed Joan down the drive at a trot. I didn't register anything she was saying until I saw the bird.

The small grassland prairie was hedged on every side by woodlands and a weird gunmetal-gray sky above that had lost the dimension of depth entirely; just a flat, pearlescent lid screwed down over top of the world. The eagle was hurt badly. It looked like it had fallen out of the sky and got hung up in the brush, like time and motion had stopped immediately before impact. Its wings were bent in the middle like a hand-painted graphic of a killer bird dive-bombing the earth for good.

What was there, what was *really* there in the grass, breathing shallow labored breaths wasn't an icon, though. What was *really* there was the emotional inverse of all that and one of the most grotesque things I've ever seen. We walked up to the vaguely cruciform posture of a mature, male, American bald eagle, splayed out, inverted, and tangled up unmoving amongst the prairie grass. When the bird raised its perfectly white head we saw that its eyes were shut tight beneath a white paste, like someone had scraped and filleted a fish, then slathered its offal over the eagle's eyes, gluing them shut un-majestic. The eagle opened its mouth some and wagged his head back and forth like it was hung on a hinge. Eyes shut tight. Terrified, willful, helpless, and blind.

I turned away with my hand over my mouth mumbling "oh god oh god oh god oh god oh god oh god" repeatedly and compulsively like a bag lady. John Michael said somebody should call 411 and that seemed directed at me. He said 411 and that seemed appropriate because what the fuck do you do when an eagle crashes in the yard? You need some information. Here's all the information I had at that moment about the American Bald Eagle: Eagles are said to have excellent eye-sight; on the short list of animals to be chosen as the symbolic referent for the newly formed United States of America, the bald eagle came in just above the wild turkey which was Ben Franklin's top choice; the tufts of graying hair in the center of my chest form this convincing silhouette of a bird with its head turned to one side, like the crest of the Hohenzollerns or some U.S. War Bonds logo;

the eagle tasked with eating Prometheus' liver every day for eternity was named Altair. But this Bald eagle, the one dying in front of us, was not any of those. He was not the silhouette on my chest. He was not selling war bonds. He was not an icon or a myth or any other link on the chain of signification. The eagle wasn't a story or a symbol: he was an individual and was badly injured.

The animal jumped now and again, trying to figure out how to clear himself of the mess, how to get back to where he came from. He shifted and found purchase on the ground where he stood almost at full height, still slumped somehow, but fully three feet high. His crown feathers were white. There wasn't a fleck of anything but white in his crown.

The next hour was queer and sad and beautiful. Joan, John Michael and I were a perfectly balanced confederation of individuals; we did only what came most naturally to us in response to the situation, and each of those responses was appropriate. John Michael prayed, Joanie sang, and I called directory assistance.

I turned around and walked away, like how you walk away from a table when you're going to make a phone call because it would be rude to talk on the phone next to a dying bald eagle. I started making calls and using the internet function on my phone to try and get somebody on the horn who knew what to do. If I am sometimes a little bit dull, I make up for it with an equally blunt persistence. I got hold of some 411 operator in another part of the state.

"Directory assistance how…."

"Hi, I'm outside of Leland Michigan and I'm sitting here with this bald eagle that, like, crashed or something. I think it just fell out of the sky. I need to get some help for this bird. It's hurt very badly."

"I'm sorry sir. Where are you?"

"Leland Michigan"

" ….."

"Leland…"

"Sir, I don't even know where that is…"

"Well ma'am, do you have a computer in front of you?"

"Yes. I've got like five of them…."

"Okay, then look it up. I need you to help me."

"I'm up in Arenac County, I don't even know where you are."

"Ma'am I'm asking you to help me. I need you to try harder to help me, please."

"Sir you need to call the 911 dispatcher in your area"

This struck me as a very sensible idea, and helpful, so I did. The emergency dispatcher had the Department of Natural Resources on the phone in a heartbeat, patched me over, and I spoke with them directly. It was a Saturday, and I could tell that the DNR officer, Rebecca was her name, was putting on her boots as we spoke. She said she'd be there in an hour.

John Michael was kneeling in the prairie grass when I got back. The dried husks of bolted wildflowers—just grown and already ending—crackled amongst the tender green of what was in season and next in line. In a healthy ecosystem plants don't vie for space. Each takes a turn and every season makes a calico. John Michael had his eyes closed, too. He placed his hands on his knees and turned up to the sky in a gesture equally meditative and petitioning. John Michael is something of a shaman and a pilgrim. By this I mean that he's dedicated himself to a slow path of understanding his world and any others he may encounter, and experiencing what it's like to be human those worlds with as few preconceptions as possible. He teaches outdoor education—more like outdoor perception, or How to Be Outside 101—to people who are usually just passing through. He listens to birds, goes shoeless most of the time, tracks animals in the woods, hunts with a bow he made, brain-tans his hides, the whole shooting match. He has an intentionality, an honest clarity of purpose, that I admire and, in my weaker moments, envy.

The driveway was laid with number nine gravel, the bigger stuff that covers itself in its own dust and sometimes takes a dull shine in the light. Joanie stood about eight feet from her brother and the bird. She was wearing her big, red, down parka. A few winters ago, she took and sewed a patch—a rainbow quilt pattern—over the brand name stitched onto the jacket. It looks better than the logo, and I always thought it was cool that she did that. I walked back up and stood next to her. She crossed her arms in front of her the way people do when they're going to be somewhere for a minute; her hair was tangled up from the wind or the distress. She was singing or humming a series of low, arpeggiated notes in repetition, maybe three or four. If anything is as arresting as the unadorned beauty of Joan's voice it's the endless, calm gathering of melodies she shepherds. They wander somewhere inside of, or very close to her, and each melody that passes her lips is a thing so near to memory that you want to clutch it close, lest it get away again for good this time. Imagine that: melodies you want to hold because you've known them, and can't stand to let them escape you again. You might think to say that Joan has a gift, and that's partly true; it's not something everyone can do, singing like that. More than the gift of a lovely voice, though, she makes herself available to song, and the miracle is one of a vessel that is never empty.

I was shaking and, more than singing with Joan, I was moaning a bent harmony. We were making music for the bird, at the bird I guess. Let me assure you, this is not something either of us does frequently, but it was clearly, *very clearly*, the right thing to do. When you find yourself singing at odd, critical moments, and when you recognize beyond reproach that singing is the appropriate act in that moment, you'll cry a little. Every damn time.

After we'd sung to the bird for a while we were all silent. It had moved a few times but had become silent, too. Joan did some cursory iPhone research on avian botulism and its effects. Terminal dehydration is what kills them, so I dripped water out of my hand onto the bird. It craned its neck, stuck out a pale, pink dagger of a tongue and took some. He flapped around fearfully then, so I stopped.

Then I tried to heal the bird by channeling energy from the universe like a Jedi or something from a fucking Philip K. Dick novel. I visualized a pink beam of energy, about as big around as a two liter of Sprite, shooting from space, through my cranium and into my spine. I stored up the energy in my body until I had enough—there's not really any metric for this sort of thing, you just feel it out. I redirected the energy and shot a pink laser out of my belly right at the eagle. He jumped a couple of feet in the air like he'd been shocked. This is factual. Later on, Joan and John Michael would both report having performed similar maneuvers.

The DNR arrived in a black Toyota 4x4 pick up about an hour later. Rebecca wore the type of militaristic dress—black cargo pants tucked into black leather and nylon boots, black straps and black epaulettes everywhere—that has become the de riguer uniform of just about every government employee in the country. Pretty soon the lady who takes your checks at the DMV counter will come to work dressed in fatigues. Rebecca was kind, though. She wasn't a jackbooted storm trooper; she was the person I'd called, the person who had come to help us. The towel she grabbed from the bed of the truck wasn't a towel a person would use to dry their body after a shower; the terry-cloth was worn down to nibs. It was a towel for drying a dog, cleaning up a large spill, or grabbing a bald eagle out of some prairie grass. Rebecca walked up to the bird. Confidently, swiftly and carefully she scooped up the Eagle in one movement. His eyes were still shut tight. As she lifted him from the ground, the eagle's head sank down pitifully and a cascade of water—totally clear, as if distilled—fell from his mouth and nose.

In The Night

We navigate by light that is generated inside of stars, the sun, a fire, a swinging lantern: the inhabitable world takes its form in reflections whose light-source is somewhere else. The planets and their satellites, which, in our eyes, behave so similarly to the stars, are really just reflectors of some other, unmediated light. The moon is a body in a borrowed gown. While the shapes and shadows we see in our eyes have some immutable similarity to the world, those electro-chemical pulses of information are not the things of the world themselves. They are representations of forms. We're watching shadows in the cave of our own skulls.

Looking at the stars on a clear night in the country, the following question is invariably asked: "Which one's the pole star again?" It's as if once this has been established, every other cosmological particular will sort itself out in a sieve of easy azimuths and parallaxes; our position and heading in the universe revealed as though we were looking straight at the lighthouse on a sea becalmed.

I have a tendency to appear certain and correct on matters about which I feel I should be certain and correct; this even when I am practically ignorant. Let us take the position of the Pole Star as one good example: it's never the big showy one you look at first. It's never ever that one. Inasmuch as a burning gaseous inferno which is—by orders of magnitude—more distant from us than our sun can be modest, the Pole Star, seen from this planet, is a modest body. It's always the last one on the handle of the Little Dipper. Every time. Let that be your guide. Or let your iPhone be your guide.

The three of us were out on the drive, right around where we would find the eagle the next day. We came out to walk the dogs and ended up laying down, looking at the sky. There aren't many parcels of solid ground left on this planet where a person can look up and get an eyeball-full of cosmos. If, in the middle of the ocean, say, there is one hundred percent clarity of vision in this matter, I bet Leelanau County hangs in at around sixty percent. We were dutifully awestruck.

Joan had a new app on her phone, it's like a miracle. You move the phone around in front of the sky and it shows you a map of all the stars, their names and the constellations to which they belong. Fire up another browser page and you can look up the mythological particulars attendant to those constellations, connect the dots, put the stories where they go. Names and symbols and narratives were assigned to what was formerly just a field of light reaching us thousands of years after it was reflected. The light generated in the phone was reaching us instantaneously but carried with it thousands of years of mythical/historical/scientific information.

As we waved the phone around, names flashed in front of us so quickly that they were indecipherable. One of those words would have been Altair, the name of the eagle who tortured Prometheus for the crime of stealing fire. The same fire that has allowed humans to cast shadows, tell stories, sing against the dark, and be individuals in the warmth and light of a group.

Sometimes the names of Gods and stars and titans changed abruptly, flashing from the Roman to the Greek. It was glitchy, miraculous, impenetrable, and unsatisfying. We had a viewfinder to tell us where things were in the universe, show us where we stood in relation, and describe the story of our movements in time. We had a map describing both the territory and how we arrived there, but it didn't work right. It was too accurate, too much to see at once. In the end, we turned it off and laid down on the gravel drive. Satisfied, after all, to look out at the territory itself, in the moment, unconcerned with how we'd gotten there or when it would be time to go.

End

C&R PRESS CHAPBOOKS

C&R Press hosts two chapbook selection periods from June to September and November to March coupled with a reading in New York City each year. The Winter Soup Bowl and Summer Tide Pool Chapbook Series are open to new and established writers in poetry, fiction, essay and other creative writing.

2017 WINTER SOUP BOWL SELECTIONS

Heredity and Other Inventions
by Sharona Muir

On Innacuracy
by Joe Manning

2016 Summer Tide Pool

Cuntstruck
by Kate Northrop

Relief Map
by Erin M. Bertram

Love Undefined
by Jonathan Katz

2016 Winter Soup Bowl

Notes from the Negro Side of the Moon
by Earl Braggs

A Hunger Called Music: A Verse History in Black Music
by Meredith Nnoka

OTHER C&R PRESS TITLES

FICTION

Ivy vs. Dogg
by Brian Leung

A History of the Cat In Nine Chapters or Less
by Anis Shivani

While You Were Gone
by Sybil Baker

Spectrum
by Martin Ott

That Man in Our Lives
by Xu Xi

SHORT FICTION

Meditations on the Mother Tongue
by An Tran

The Protester Has Been Released
by Janet Sarbanes

ESSAY AND CREATIVE NONFICTION

Immigration Essays
by Sybil Baker

Je suis l'autre: Essays and Interrogations
by Kristina Marie Darling

Death of Art
by Chris Campanioni

POETRY

Negro Side of the Moon
by Early Braggs

Holdfast
by Christian Anton Gerard

Ex Domestica
by E.G. Cunningham

Collected Lies and Love Poems
by John Reed

Imagine Not Drowning
by Kelli Allen

Les Fauves
by Barbara Crooker

Tall as You are Tall Between Them
by Annie Christain

The Couple Who Fell to Earth
by Michelle Bitting

CHAPBOOKS

Heredity and Other Inventions by Sharona Muir
Cuntstruck by Kate Northrop
Relief Map by Erin Bertram
Love Undefined by Jonathan Katz
Ugly Love: Notes from the Negro Side of the Moon by Earl Braggs
A Hunger Called Music: A Verse History in Black Music
by Meredith Nnoka

www.ingramcontent.com/pod-product-compliance
Lightning Source LLC
Chambersburg PA
CBHW021340290326
41933CB00038B/997